Fragile MOUNTAINS

BY PAULA HOGAN

ENVIRONMENT ALERT!

Gareth Stevens Children's Books
MILWAUKEE

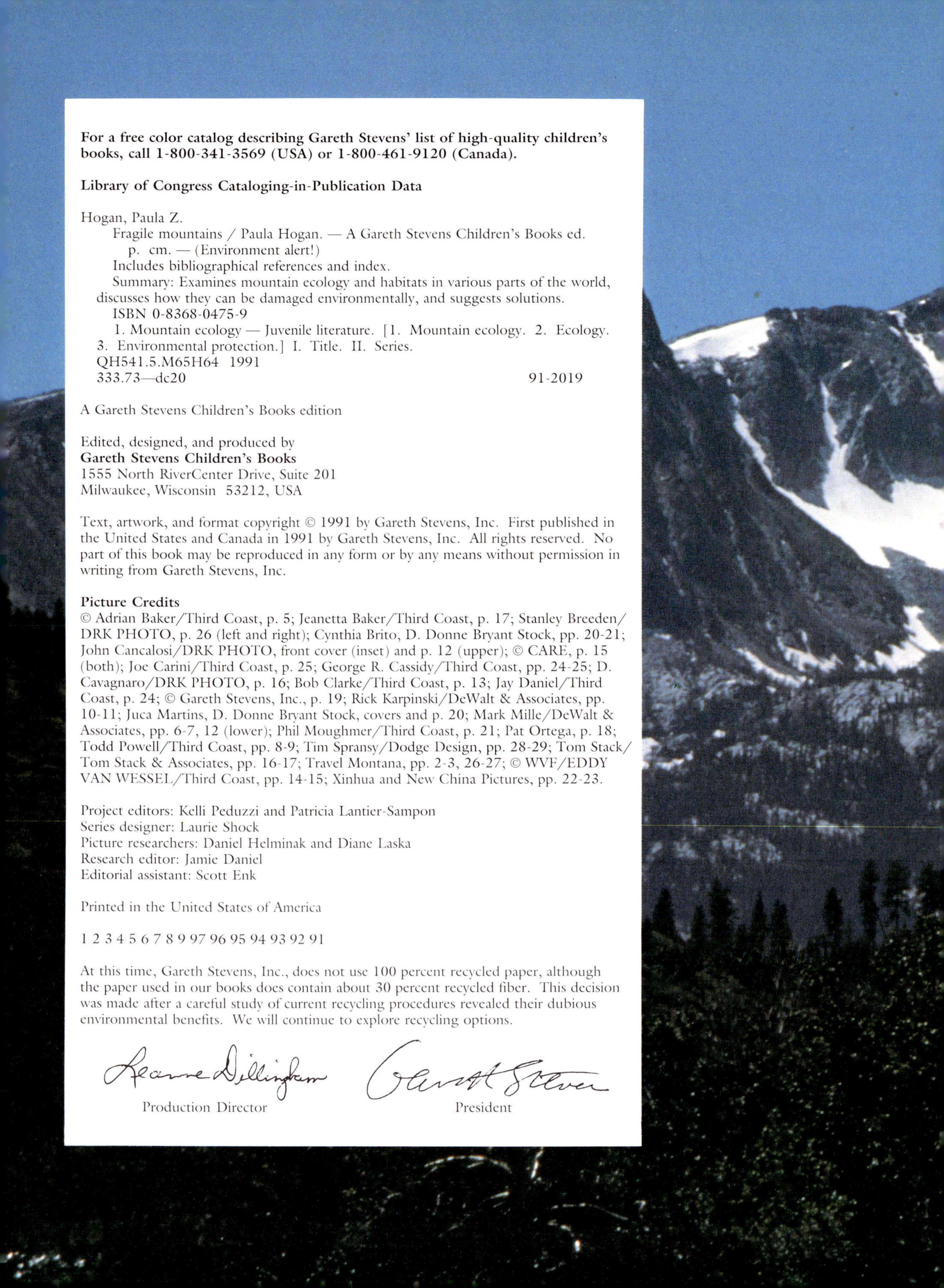

For a free color catalog describing Gareth Stevens' list of high-quality children's books, call 1-800-341-3569 (USA) or 1-800-461-9120 (Canada).

Library of Congress Cataloging-in-Publication Data

Hogan, Paula Z.
Fragile mountains / Paula Hogan. — A Gareth Stevens Children's Books ed.
p. cm. — (Environment alert!)
Includes bibliographical references and index.
Summary: Examines mountain ecology and habitats in various parts of the world, discusses how they can be damaged environmentally, and suggests solutions.
ISBN 0-8368-0475-9
1. Mountain ecology — Juvenile literature. [1. Mountain ecology. 2. Ecology. 3. Environmental protection.] I. Title. II. Series.
QH541.5.M65H64 1991
333.73—dc20 91-2019

A Gareth Stevens Children's Books edition

Edited, designed, and produced by
Gareth Stevens Children's Books
1555 North RiverCenter Drive, Suite 201
Milwaukee, Wisconsin 53212, USA

Picture Credits
© Adrian Baker/Third Coast, p. 5; Jeanetta Baker/Third Coast, p. 17; Stanley Breeden/DRK PHOTO, p. 26 (left and right); Cynthia Brito, D. Donne Bryant Stock, pp. 20-21; John Cancalosi/DRK PHOTO, front cover (inset) and p. 12 (upper); © CARE, p. 15 (both); Joe Carini/Third Coast, p. 25; George R. Cassidy/Third Coast, pp. 24-25; D. Cavagnaro/DRK PHOTO, p. 16; Bob Clarke/Third Coast, p. 13; Jay Daniel/Third Coast, p. 24; © Gareth Stevens, Inc., p. 19; Rick Karpinski/DeWalt & Associates, pp. 10-11; Juca Martins, D. Donne Bryant Stock, covers and p. 20; Mark Mille/DeWalt & Associates, pp. 6-7, 12 (lower); Phil Moughmer/Third Coast, p. 21; Pat Ortega, p. 18; Todd Powell/Third Coast, pp. 8-9; Tim Spransy/Dodge Design, pp. 28-29; Tom Stack/Tom Stack & Associates, pp. 16-17; Travel Montana, pp. 2-3, 26-27; © WVF/EDDY VAN WESSEL/Third Coast, pp. 14-15; Xinhua and New China Pictures, pp. 22-23.

Project editors: Kelli Peduzzi and Patricia Lantier-Sampon
Series designer: Laurie Shock
Picture researchers: Daniel Helminak and Diane Laska
Research editor: Jamie Daniel
Editorial assistant: Scott Enk

Printed in the United States of America

1 2 3 4 5 6 7 8 9 97 96 95 94 93 92 91

At this time, Gareth Stevens, Inc., does not use 100 percent recycled paper, although the paper used in our books does contain about 30 percent recycled fiber. This decision was made after a careful study of current recycling procedures revealed their dubious environmental benefits. We will continue to explore recycling options.

Production Director

President

CONTENTS

Words that appear in the glossary are printed in **boldface** type the first time they appear in the text.

ISLANDS IN THE SKY

Mountains are islands in the sky. Like life on real islands surrounded by water, life on a mountain is quite different from life in the surrounding lowlands. Many mountain plants and animals survive only at high **altitudes**.

A mountain must be at least 1,000 feet (305 m) tall. Anything lower is a hill. Few mountains stand alone. Usually, they are grouped together in ranges. In some places, mountain peaks are joined together by ridges, or they are separated by deep canyons.

Mountains are storehouses of **natural resources**. Yet for thousands of years, they remained almost untouched. Today, mountains are in trouble. Many people are making fortunes by **damming** mountain streams, mining, lumbering, and building. By doing this, they damage the fragile mountain **environment**. Air and water **pollution**, soil **erosion**, harm to wildlife, and human overcrowding are several results of the greedy scramble for mountain resources. If we do not save the mountains, nothing will be able to live in them.

Opposite: The Tyrol in Austria is part of the Alps.

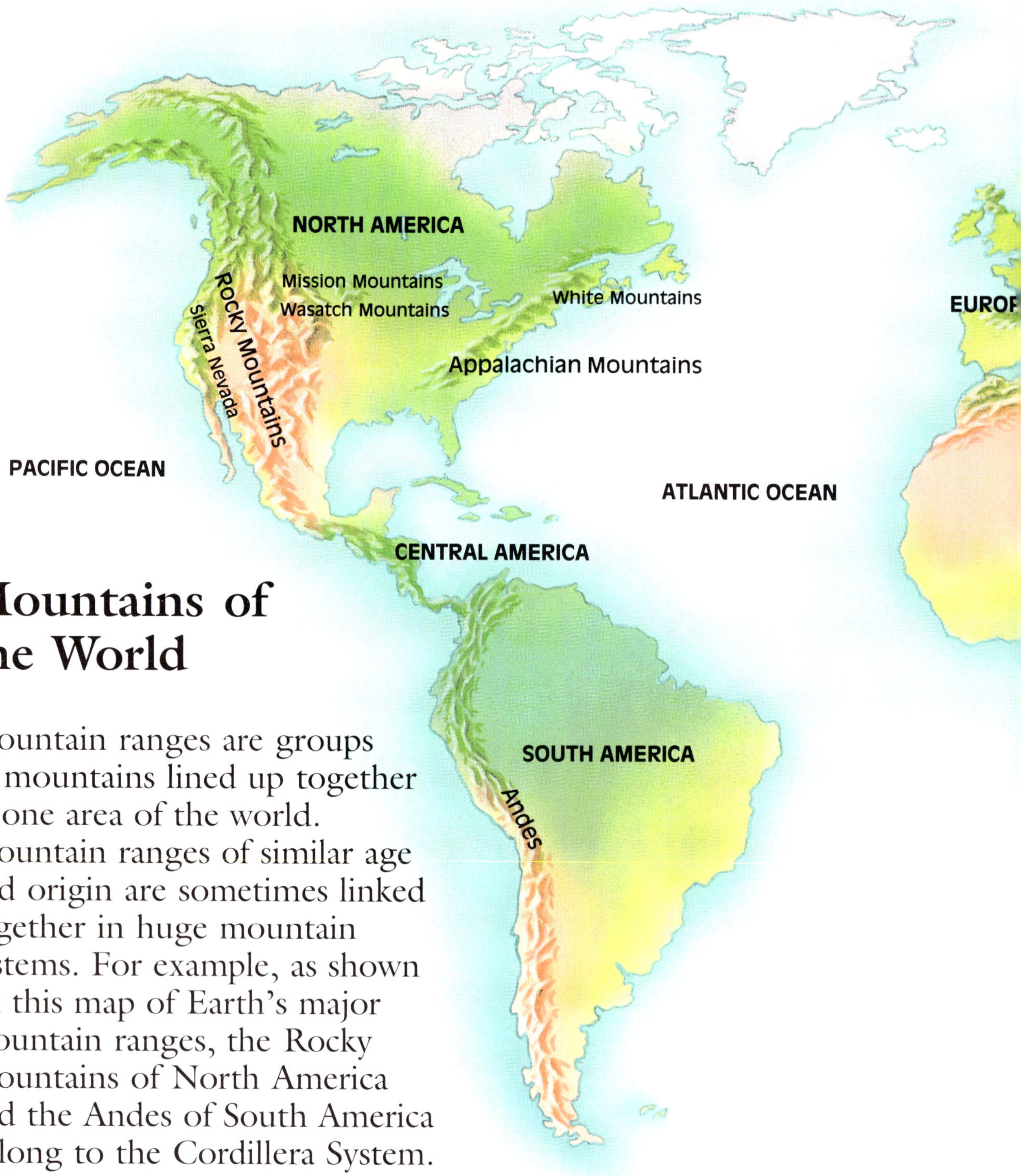

Mountains of the World

Mountain ranges are groups of mountains lined up together in one area of the world. Mountain ranges of similar age and origin are sometimes linked together in huge mountain systems. For example, as shown on this map of Earth's major mountain ranges, the Rocky Mountains of North America and the Andes of South America belong to the Cordillera System. This system is part of a larger system known as the "Ring of Fire" that circles the Pacific Ocean, so called because of its many volcanoes.

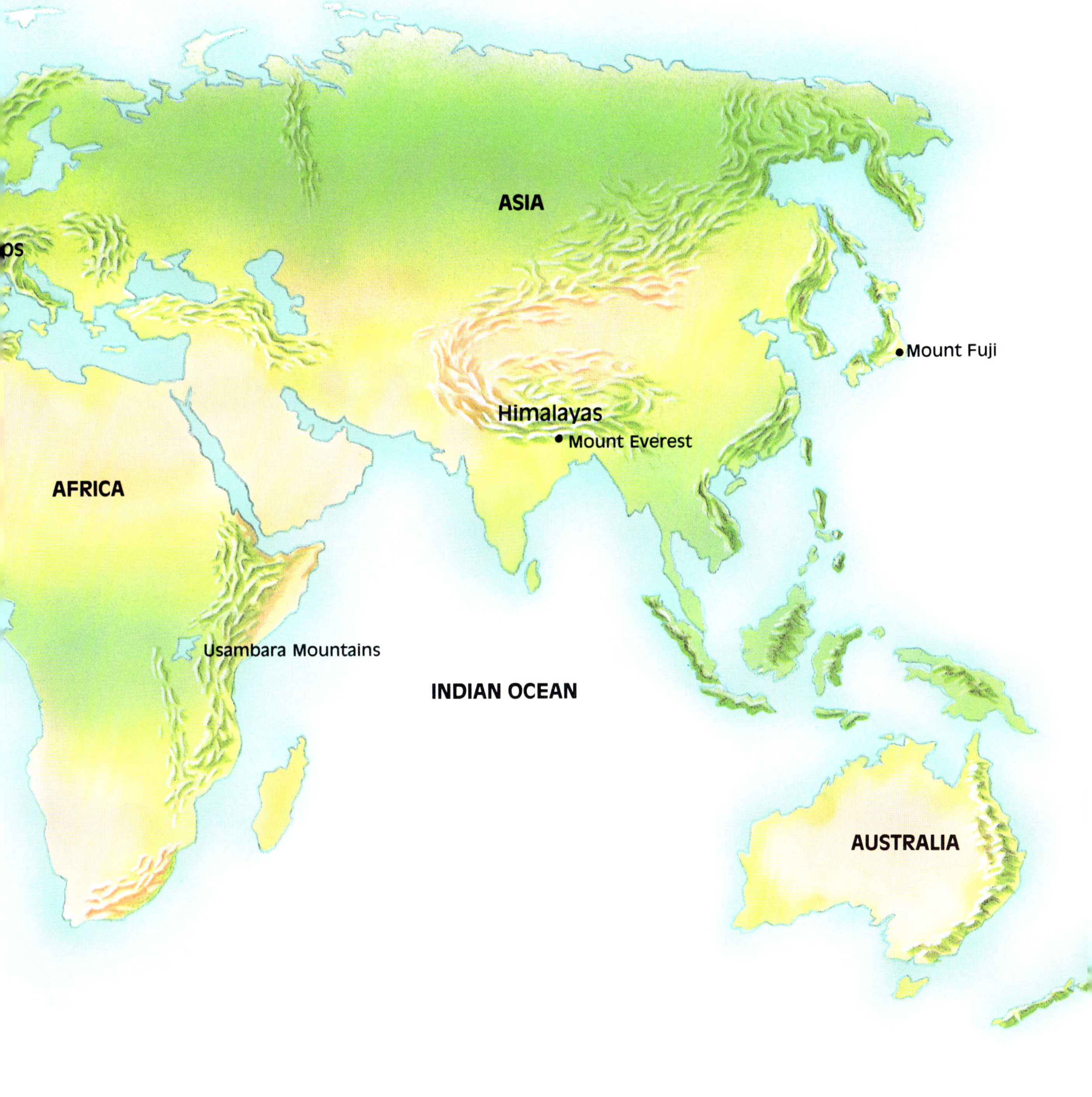
os
ASIA
Mount Fuji
Himalayas
Mount Everest
AFRICA
Usambara Mountains
INDIAN OCEAN
AUSTRALIA

The Zones of Life

In the mountains, every small gain in altitude is like traveling a few hundred miles closer to the North Pole. Plants and animals living at the base of a mountain cannot live on its freezing peaks. Each **species** must stay in its own temperature zone to survive.

Plants at the bases of mountains are much like those in the surrounding lowlands. On the middle slopes, both hardwoods and pine trees grow, while only pines grow on the cold higher slopes. The **timberline** is the point where it is too cold and windy for any trees to grow. The highest mountains are treeless at the top, and only a few arctic grasses can grow on these peaks.

Seed-eating birds, such as grouse, must stay in the zone where their food grows. Many animals live in the aspen groves and pine forests, where food is plentiful. Some mountain animals, such as deer and bears, can live at almost any altitude. The pika, a kind of rabbit, is one of the few animals that lives above the timberline all year round.

This photograph of the Ten Mile Range in Breckenridge, Colorado, clearly shows the different zones of life possible in a single landscape. From grasslands to shrubs to forests to snowy mountaintops, various plants and animals thrive in the temperatures most suited to their individual needs.

Mountains at Risk

Mountain regions hold a storehouse of riches. Enormous forests provide lumber for building and wood for paper. Precious metals, oil, and gas provide raw materials and fuel for industries and homes. Mountain streams provide water for crop **irrigation**. And the beautiful mountains themselves provide a lovely place to live or vacation. But the careless use of these riches causes all

People are finding more and more ways to use the natural resources of the mountains. Some of these ways, shown below, may damage the environment.

sorts of environmental damage. Air pollution and lumber harvesting cause **deforestation**, which in turn causes soil erosion. Mining pollutes mountain streams with chemical wastes. Damming drowns entire mountain environments. And as more people move to the mountains to work and live, they change the landscape and endanger the animals.

If we do not take steps to control pollution and the destruction of animal **habitats**, the mountain environments will not survive. All that will be left are bare peaks, where nothing can live.

FACT FILE
Crisis in the Himalayas

For thousands of years, the Himalaya Mountains of Nepal remained almost untouched. Farmers planted crops in small, terraced fields and let their livestock graze in mountain pastures. But modern times brought drastic changes to Nepal, and these changes began to destroy the environment.

Nepal's population grew as modern medicines saved many lives. More homes had to be built, so many more trees were cut for lumber and firewood. With extra mouths to feed, farmers cleared forests to have more fields in which to grow food.

Airplane travel brought many mountain climbers and foreign tourists to Nepal. Huge forests were cut each year to provide firewood for them as well. In fact, tourists played a big part in spoiling the beautiful scenery that they were coming to see!

The Giant Panda

The giant panda once thrived in the **bamboo** forests of China's mountains. Today, only a few pandas are left. Why? Mainly because the bamboo, the pandas' only food, is being cleared for human settlement.

Below: The Himalayas cross many national boundaries. Ecological damage by one country can affect others, too. For example, cutting trees in Nepal causes terrible flooding in nearby Bangladesh.

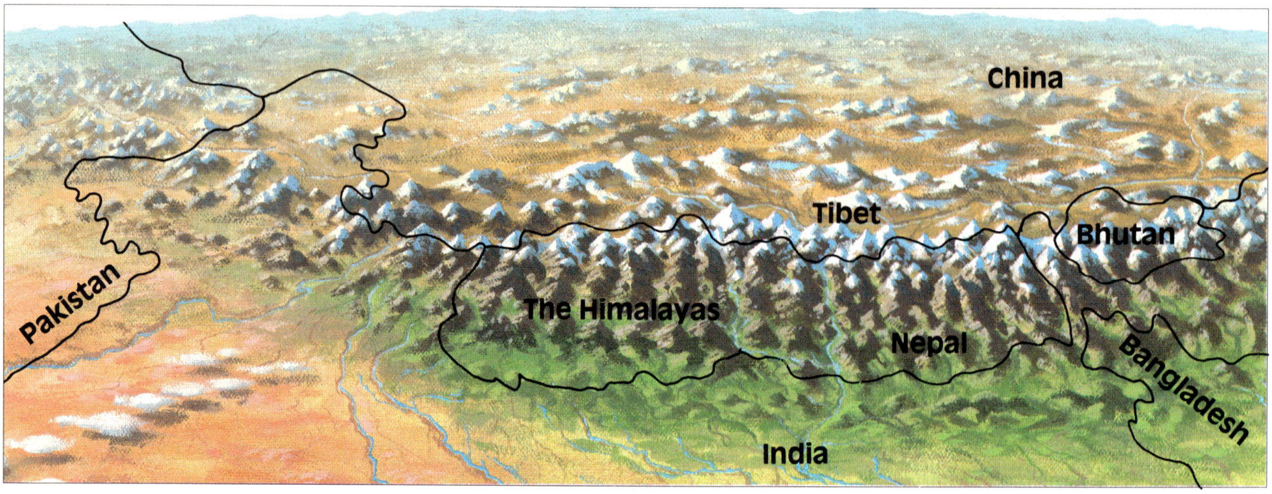

Above: The number of people in Nepal will reach 30 million by the year 2000. To raise enough food for them, farmers clear forests for cropland. Such heavy logging has destroyed many forests.

The loss of so much forest land had tragic consequences for Nepal. Without tree roots to hold the soil in place, it washed off the slopes and into rivers. In some areas, only bare rock was left, and no plants could grow.

Deforestation also caused terrible floods. Rainwater that was once absorbed by tree roots ran into the rivers, which then overflowed their banks. In 1987, the Ganges River overflowed as it ran down from the Himalayas. The flood drowned hundreds of people in two of Nepal's neighbors, India and Bangladesh.

Nepal's government is replanting, but some **conservationists** fear that this is too little, too late. Not enough trees are being planted, and it will take many years for them to grow up. Meanwhile, some government workers who are supposed to protect Nepal's forests are selling trees to lumber companies.

Below: A peaceful sunset in Nepal casts its shadow over endangered Himalayan forests.

Right, top: Many people lost their homes and lives when rain in the Himalayas rushed down deforested slopes and caused terrible flooding in the rivers of Bangladesh.

Right, bottom: A CARE volunteer helps give out food to flood victims.

The destruction of Nepal's mountain forests has left the country with an uncertain future as it tries to cope with the drastic changes in the environment. With more careful use of its resources, this crisis might have been avoided or made less severe.

PROTECTING THE MOUNTAINS

Cleaning Up the Air

In Europe and North America, air pollution is killing both the mountain forests and people. The pollution comes from car exhaust, factory smokestacks, wood-burning stoves, and coal-burning power plants. Steep mountain valleys trap polluted air, making pollution even worse.

Air pollution weakens trees, causing the needles and leaves to die. Pollution gets into the soil and prevents tree roots from absorbing **nutrients** and water. People suffer, too. Those living in mountain cities such as Denver, Colorado, have their lives shortened by months or even years from breathing the polluted air.

Air pollution can be controlled. In Denver, the use of wood-burning stoves is banned on high-pollution days. In winter, when cold air makes pollution worse, Denver drivers must use cleaner-burning gasoline in their cars. The Swiss government is also reducing air pollution in the Alps by putting trucks on trains and hauling them over mountain passes. These trains are powered by electricity and don't emit polluting fumes.

The Lost Butterflies

Dust churned up by trucks and cars on dirt roads also pollutes the air. Traffic dust may be the reason that so many butterflies have disappeared from the mountains.

Left: A layer of thick smog covers Denver, Colorado. Cities along the front range of the Rocky Mountains suffer more and more from this brown cloud of air pollution.

Above: Trains are used in the Swiss Alps to cut down on the number of cars and trucks in the mountains. This helps reduce pollution.

Above: The spotted owl is endangered because its forest home in the mountains of the northwestern United States is being destroyed by logging. Conservationists are working to stop the tree cutting.

Protecting Highland Forests

Air pollution kills thousands of trees each year, but logging kills millions of them. In China, Indonesia, the Philippines, and Thailand, mountains are stripped of their trees, which are used for lumber and paper.

Many mountainsides are clear-cut — every tree is chopped down. These barren patches spoil the beauty of the mountains and cause soil erosion. On certain slopes, new trees can never grow back. Even when lumber companies replant, the forest is never the same. Some plants and animals that lived in the old forest never return.

Many people are working to save mountain forests. In the United States, conservation groups have saved thousands of acres of woodland and old-growth forests. The government of Nepal is planting trees and paying villagers to pen their livestock so that mountain pastures can grow back. Climbers must use **kerosene** stoves instead of firewood. In the Usambara Mountains of Tanzania, the International Union for Conservation of Nature teaches people how to use the forests without destroying them. These projects include harvesting beans from wild coffee plants and setting up nature reserves.

A girl of the mountains of Costa Rica plants a tree to help prevent soil erosion.

Above: Gold mining in the mountains of Brazil has polluted this river in the Amazon rain forest and killed the trees at the river's edge.

Left: The Serra Pelada gold mine in the mountains of Brazil has totally destroyed the lush rain forest.

Stopping Mining Pollution

Mountains often have precious minerals buried below their surfaces. To get these minerals, miners tunnel deep inside the mountain, harming the environment in the process. They sometimes hollow out entire mountains, causing them to collapse. Chemicals and mining wastes pile up outside the mine. Dust from these wastes blows about and poisons the air. Rain washes mining wastes into rivers and lakes, killing the fish and making the water unfit to drink.

Recently, some people have tried to stop mining pollution. In Utah, conservationists are battling the mining, oil, and gas companies by trying to limit the number of roads the companies can build in the Slick Rock area. In Alaska, conservation groups have forced some small gold mines to shut down. The miners were dumping dirt and chemicals into the streams, causing over 80 percent of Alaska's water pollution.

Right: To get at minerals and truck them out, roads are built through the mountain wilderness. Road building destroys the fragile plants and soil. The roar of machinery frightens away wildlife.

Flooding the Wilderness

Damming a mountain river provides water for irrigation and household use. Water fills the valley, creating a huge lake, or **reservoir**, behind the dam.

Opposite: When a dam across China's Chang Jiang is finished, the water behind the dam will rise, covering much of the beautiful and famous Three Gorges area.

But the damage that dams do is a big price to pay for extra water. Beautiful mountain scenery disappears underwater. Plants drown, and wildlife is driven out. Even trout and other fish that once swam in the swiftly moving river cannot live in a still lake.

Some rivers in mountain areas have been saved by conservation groups and concerned citizens. In Longmont, Colorado, for example, voters and conservation groups convinced the city government not to build a dam on the North Saint Vrain River.

Below: The dam across the Chang Jiang will generate electricity, but it will also change the course of the river and harm fish and other wildlife downstream.

Controlling Human Damage

More and more people are choosing to live or vacation in the mountains. More roads, restaurants, houses, and hotels create more water and air pollution in the mountain environment. The people crowd out the animals. In the Wasatch Mountains of Utah, over 40,000 mule deer starved one winter because their grazing range had been replaced by houses.

Thousands of trees are cut to make room for ski lifts and runs. For better skiing, bulldozers reshape the mountain slopes. This destroys the plant cover and speeds up erosion. But little has been done to stop the destruction of fragile mountain areas.

Hikers also damage mountain slopes. In the White Mountains of New Hampshire, hikers have trampled over endangered plants. Now, however, many wilderness areas in the United States have well-marked hiking trails. Signs tell hikers to stay on the trail and take their trash with them.

Left: Hikers rest on a trail in the Sierra Nevada of California.

Above: The mountains are favorite places for skiers, but skiing and other recreation in the mountains may harm the delicate balance of nature. Skiers pack down the snow as they whiz down the mountain, crushing the plants and grasses underneath.

Left: Some Japanese now call their sacred Mount Fuji "the Great Garbage Can in the Sky." On weekends, as many as 50,000 people, many of them tourists, hike to the top. They leave soda cans, food wrappers, and other trash along the way.

Left, both: The beautiful Impeyan pheasant and the musk deer have returned to the Himalaya Mountains since a national park was created near Mount Everest.

Above: Montana's Mission Mountains are protected. Such conservation may be the only way to save mountain environments.

Keeping the Mountains Wild

The best way to save mountains is to turn them into national parks, where there are few roads and no dams, mining, or lumbering. Fortunately, more and more mountain land is being protected. Governments are passing laws to control pollution. Conservation groups are working to save mountain forests.

Native Americans in Montana's Mission Mountains set aside over 89,000 acres (36,000 ha) of land as a wilderness area. Peru set up reserves in the Andes to safeguard the endangered vicuña. Ever since Nepal created Sagarmatha National Park around Mount Everest, some endangered animals have come back.

We cannot turn all mountains into parks, so we must use mountain resources carefully. Lumber companies must cut trees in areas that can be replanted. Miners must avoid polluting air and water. Dams should be built only when they are really necessary. Homes and vacation resorts should be built only in specially planned areas. If we treat the mountains gently, their beautiful scenery and wildlife will survive for everyone to enjoy.

RESEARCH ACTIVITIES

1. **Learn more about erosion.**
   Fill two shallow pans with soil. Plant one with grass seed, and leave the other one bare. Water the seeds gently every two days, keeping the pans in a sunny spot. When the grass is nice and thick, hold the two pans at a slant. Carefully pour water down the center of each pan. What happens to the grassy soil compared with the plain soil? Which pan loses more soil to water erosion?

2. **Collect samples of the plants where you live.**
   (Be careful not to trespass on private property or pick any endangered species.) Can any of them survive in the mountains? Observe the animals in your area. Which of these might live in the mountains as well?

3. **Find out how different kinds of garbage pollute mountain soil.**
Fill a dishpan or large bucket with soil. In the soil, bury an apple core, a plastic bag, an aluminum soda can, a chicken bone, and some leaves. Water the soil once a week. After three months, dig up the things you buried. What has happened to them? Describe the changes. Which of the things you buried will stay around a long time as garbage?

Things You Can Do to Help

The following activities will help protect the mountains. Try to involve your friends, family, and classmates in your conservation efforts.

1. **Conserve electricity.** We get electricity by burning coal, damming rivers, and operating dangerous nuclear power plants. To cut down on the use of fuels taken from mountains, contact your local power company and ask how you can conserve electricity at home and at school.

2. **Save the trees.** Many mountain forests are cut down to make paper. Help your community save trees by recycling paper. Write on both sides of a piece of paper. Bring cloth tote bags to the grocery store instead of using paper ones. Reuse cardboard boxes. Make a list of other ways to save paper, and post this list in your classroom.

Places to Write for More Information

The following organizations work to save mountain environments. When you write to them for more information, be specific about what you want to know.

Alliance for the Wild Rockies
415 N. Higgins Avenue
Missoula, Montana 59802

Southern Utah Wilderness Alliance
P.O. Box 518
Cedar City, Utah 84721

World Wildlife Fund (Canada)
90 Eglinton Avenue East, Suite 504
Toronto, Ontario M4P 2Z

More Books to Read

Disastrous Volcanoes, by Melvin Berger (Franklin Watts)
Mountains, by Brian McIntyre (Dial Press)
One Day in the Alpine Tundra, by Jean Craighead George (Crowell)
Project Panda Watch, by Miriam Schlein (Atheneum)

Glossary

altitude — the height above sea level

bamboo — a giant, woody, tropical plant

conservationist — a person who works to protect nature

damming — building a barrier across a river or stream to hold back water

deforestation — the clearing of an area of trees

environment — the surroundings in which animals, plants, and other living things live

erosion — the wearing away of land by wind, water, or other forces

habitat — an environment where plants and animals live and grow

irrigation — the supplying of water to crops using ditches or pipes

kerosene — a kind of fuel similar to gasoline

mountain — a point of land at least 1,000 feet (305 m) tall

natural resources — things occurring in nature, such as trees, fertile soil, or minerals, that can be used in producing goods

nutrient — a substance needed for life and growth

pollution — the spoiling of air, soil, or water with poisonous wastes or garbage

reservoir — a huge lake in which water is stored for human use

species — a group of living things with the same physical characteristics

timberline — the height on a mountain above which it is too cold for trees to grow

Index

[redacted]

[redacted]